BRITISH MUSEUM POCKET TREASURY

Romans

INTRODUCTION

Rome's empire at its height encompassed the northern and southern shores of the Mediterranean, two-thirds of continental Europe, Britain and most of the Near East. Her power and influence lasted the better part of a millennium (the first and last objects in this book are separated by seven hundred years, and are by no means the earliest or latest which could have been chosen). As a result, the visitor who wishes to see a fully representative sample of the Roman artefacts held in the collections of the British Museum must be prepared to visit many different galleries.

Rome's origins were very humble – a scatter of huts, similar to other small settlements of the Latin people. However, under Latin and Etruscan kings and finally governed as a Republic, Rome came to control most of Italy, either through conquest or through a complex web of alliances. During the second and first centuries BC Rome became involved in incessant wars overseas and conquered vast territories throughout the Mediterranean. The subsequent flow of wealth, people and ideas into Italy transformed Roman life, but the accompanying stresses and strains within society proved too much for the political structure of the Republic, which collapsed in a series of bloody civil wars.

From this chaos emerged Augustus, the first emperor (27 BC-AD 14). As absolute ruler of the empire, in an era before mass-media, the image he projected to his subjects was all-important. The period of prosperity which his reign ushered in saw a flourishing of arts and crafts, literature and architecture; this is reflected in the collections of the Museum, where many of the finest Roman artefacts date from the early empire.

Perhaps Rome's greatest achievement was to bring together hundreds of different peoples into a single political and economic unit. Local practices, beliefs, fashions and languages often survived, but a gradual process of Romanisation took place as individuals and whole communities realised the benefits that citizenship and full integration into the Roman system could bring. Although Christianity transformed or destroyed many aspects of the classical pagan world, and internal and external political events finally brought down the empire itself, Rome nevertheless bequeathed an immense and lasting legacy.

This book serves as an introduction to some of the Roman objects in the British Museum, and hopefully it will also inspire visitors to learn more about Rome, one of the world's greatest and most influential civilisations.

SILVER COIN FROM ROME

*c.*300 BC

This silver coin shows on one side the she-wolf, nurturing Romulus the legendary founder of Rome, and his twin brother Remus. On the other side is Hercules, recognisable by his club and lion skin. However, this Hercules is beardless, with waved hair and a diadem, quite different from his usual rugged appearance, and is suggestive of the recently deified ruler of

Macedon, Alexander the Great (d.323 BC). The images on this coin clearly associate the idea of Rome (personified by the wolf and twins) with Hercules (in Rome worshipped as the god of victory) and Alexander, who conquered the lands east of the Mediterranean, bringing Greek culture to them.

During the next two centuries, Rome in its turn conquered the Mediterranean lands, and her leaders were regarded by much of the eastern Mediterranean as the successors to Alexander's kingdoms.

FREEDMEN RELIEF

30-10 BC

This is part of the funerary monument of Lucius Antistius Sarculo, a free-born Roman priest of the Salian order, whose duties were to observe the opening and closure of the military campaign season, and his wife and freedwoman (former slave) Antistia Plutia. Both busts are in the realistic style typical of the period, and it is impossible to discern the gulf in social origin of this couple from the images alone.

During the Republic, countless slaves were brought to Rome and Italy following the conquests of territories such as Spain and Greece. Many worked in agriculture or building projects, others were teachers, craftsmen such as sculptors, and potters or even cooks. Freedmen and women were given rights and privileges by Augustus, including (happily for Antistia) the right to marry Roman citizens, and their monuments proudly proclaim their full membership of Roman society.

CAMEO OF AUGUSTUS (THE BLACAS CAMEO)

c.AD 14-20

Carved from a three-layered sardonyx, this cameo, a fragment of a larger portrait, shows the emperor Augustus in majestic pose. As well as a sword-belt, symbolising his military authority, he wears the divine breast-plate (*aegis*) usually associated with the goddess Minerva. Except for the Medieval jewelled head-band, the cameo has survived unrestored.

Such a depiction of the emperor, with its open assumption of a divine attribute, was probably seen by only a few. Universal distribution could have proved very controversial, since mistrust of monarchy was still very engrained in Roman society, and many hoped for a return to the Republic. In portraits intended for a wider audience during the emperor's lifetime, such as those on coins and statues, the images portrayed are much more modest.

THE PORTLAND VASE

TURN OF THE 1ST CENTURY BC/AD

This vase, probably the finest surviving piece of cameo glass, was formed by meticulously cutting away the layer of opaque white glass with which the dark blue vase underneath had been covered. Careful variation of the depth of carving produced effects of shading and perspective with painstaking attention to detail in the figures and structures. Although the identification of the scene and its characters is uncertain, suggestions include the marriage of Peleus and Thetis, the parents of Achilles, or members of the imperial family.

The vase was discovered in a tomb on the Via Tuscolana outside Rome in 1582. From there it passed via cardinals, princes and Sir William Hamilton to the Dukes of Portland, who loaned it to the Museum, which eventually acquired it in 1945. It lacks its original tapered base, and in 1845 was smashed to pieces by a drunken visitor. The vase as seen now is the product of careful restorations, most recently in 1988-9.

Bronze Head of Augustus
(The Meroë Head)
c.27-25 BC

This head once formed part of an over life-sized statue of the emperor Augustus. The classically perfect proportions, and the emperor's calm, distant gaze, emphasised with inset eyes of glass and stone, give him an air of quiet, assured strength. Coins and statues were the main media for propagating the emperor's image and this statue, like many others throughout the empire, was a continuous reminder of the overall power of Rome and its emperor.

It was the symbolic importance of the statue that, in an unexpected way, ultimately led to the head's preservation. It was found at Meroë, in the Sudan, buried beneath the steps of a native temple dedicated to Victory. It seems likely that the head, hacked from its statue by Meroitic tribesmen during a raid on Roman Egypt, was placed there deliberately, so as to be permanently below the feet of its captors.

This detail of the tinned and gilded scabbard shows Augustus' stepson Tiberius symbolically presenting his recent victories to the emperor. Augustus is semi-nude and sits in the pose of Jupiter, flanked by Victory and Mars Ultor (Mars the Avenger), as Tiberius, in military dress, presents Augustus with a statuette of Victory. Similar scenes on coins, intended for much wider distribution, show Augustus more modestly dressed in a toga.

The iron sword and decorated bronze scabbard were found in Mainz, Germany, and were almost certainly commissioned for a senior officer to commemorate a victorious military campaign. Such campaigns were essential for the extension and protection of Rome's empire, which by the time of Augustus encompassed most of the Mediterranean basin. The symbolic act of presenting them to the emperor avoided the destructive competition between generals, which had brought down the Republic.

FELIC
ITAS
TIBE
RI

ARTEMIDORUS
EARLY 2ND CENTURY AD

This mummy-case, decorated with polychrome painting and gold leaf, was made for a young man called Artemidorus, who died in his early twenties, and was discovered at Hawara in Egypt in 1888. A cultural mix, its form and much of its decoration seem typically Egyptian, with painted scenes of the funerary ritual and deities such as Anubis, yet the inscription on the chest and the man's name are Greek, reflecting the 300-year domination of Egypt by the Greek Ptolemaic dynasty – the heirs of Alexander the Great.

Perhaps the most striking feature is the realistic portrait, a phenomenon not seen in Egypt before the Roman conquest. Approximately one thousand mummy portraits are known, most either on linen or, as here, on wood, dating from the first to the third century AD. The portraits show changing fashions in hairstyles, dress and jewellery, and also provide us with the largest group of faces of real people from the ancient world.

Funerary Relief from Palmyra

2nd Century AD

Tamma, the Palmyrene woman portrayed here, is dressed in local costume and is covered with jewellery – necklaces, brooches and bracelets – many of which are paralleled by tomb finds and sculpture from Africa, Egypt and the eastern Mediterranean. Her image, however, has a very Roman feel, and is part of the phenomenon of life-like funerary portraiture seen throughout the empire. This relief originally adorned a burial compartment (*cubiculum*), inside one of the many tower tombs around Palmyra.

Palmyra, in modern Syria, was situated on a major trade route between the Mediterranean and the Middle and Far East. Silk, perfumes, precious stones, spices and other exotic goods flowed from India, China and Arabia, and many Palmyrenes, among them perhaps Tamma's family, grew wealthy from the trade. With the peace and stability of the empire (the *pax romana*), Palmyra prospered still further.

SELECTION OF ROMAN JEWELLERY

1ST-3RD CENTURY AD

The pieces shown here are typical of the jewellery that was worn by wealthy Roman women in the early-mid empire. The solid gold pendant necklace dating to around AD 200 shows the head of Medusa, often used as a lucky charm. The gold double-sphere earrings featuring female masks on the upper part date to the second century AD, and were found together with a tiara, cameos, earrings and other jewellery in the tomb of a woman at Miletopolis in modern Turkey. The second necklace is of gold, set with amethysts, and was made in the third century AD; the amethyst settings are joined by gold links shaped as *peltae*, the shields used by the mythical female warriors, the Amazons.

Most of the Roman jewellery that has survived was found in tombs, though we have plenty of Roman representations of jewellery being worn, for example on statues, funerary reliefs and the mummy portraits of Roman Egypt.

'CLYTIE'

c.AD 40-50

This marble bust has long been known as 'Clytie', after the mythological figure who fell in love with Helios-Apollo, the sun god, and was turned into a flower which followed the sun's path across the sky. However, in spite of the leafy base of the bust, it is more likely that the woman is mortal; some believe her to be Antonia Minor, mother of the emperor Claudius (AD 41-54).

Her endearing, downcast gaze, the fine detail of her hair, and the highly sensuous effect of her drapery, have won her many admirers over the centuries. Foremost among them was the collector Charles Townley, who brought Clytie and many other fine pieces of sculpture from Rome and the surrounding area to Britain in the 1760s-80s. Following his death in 1805, Charles Townley's marbles were acquired by the British Museum, where they can still be admired as a rare example of an intact eighteenth-century collection.

PAINTED WALL-PANEL

EARLY 1ST CENTURY AD

The interior walls of wealthy Roman houses were often covered with painted decoration. Fashions in wall-painting changed over time, and examples of at least four major styles, spanning nearly three centuries, have been found. This panel formed part of a wall of a villa at Boscoreale near Pompeii, which was painted in the so-called third style, where central panels showing landscapes, still lifes such as fruit and fish, or mythological scenes were surrounded by elongated frames of columns, candelabra and floral motifs.

This particular scene shows a harbour, a very popular subject, and is painted in the simple, almost impressionist style often used in Roman landscape. A boat leaves harbour, its sail billowing in the wind, and is watched from a seaside villa by several people, one of whom raises an arm to wave goodbye. In the distance other boats can be seen, while in the foreground a man fishes from a bridge.

MOSAIC PANEL FROM POPULONIA
*c.*AD 100

This mosaic panel formed part of the floor of the dining room (*triclinium*) of a villa near Populonia, Italy. Mosaic floors, made of small, squared pieces of stone or glass (*tesserae*), became very popular during the Roman period. Central panels such as this were pre-fabricated in specialist workshops before being set into larger, plainer floors, and achieved outstanding effects through the use of ever smaller *tesserae*. Here, for example, all twelve species of sea-creatures including octopus, red mullet, scorpion fish and spiny lobster are identifiable. The subject matter of the panel shows one element of the huge range of foodstuffs which became available to wealthier Romans in the early empire. The extravagant recipes found in cookery writers such as Apicius, featuring rich sauces, rare herbs and spices, and exotic meat and fish, attest the transformation of Roman cuisine.

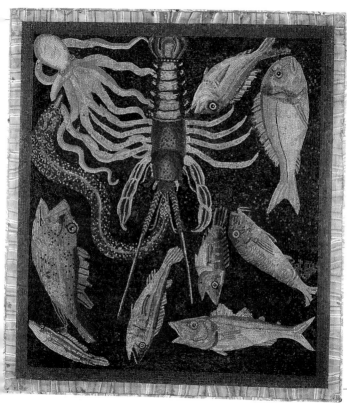

SARCOPHAGUS OF A YOUNG GIRL

c. AD 160-80

The girl lies on her funeral bed and is flanked by her parents, their hands raised to their covered heads in a gesture of grief. Mourners stand round the girl, beating their breasts, tearing their hair and raising their hands to the sky as they lament her. The pet dog crouched beneath her bed and the pair of slippers are poignant symbols of the girl's premature death.

The use of sarcophagi spread rapidly throughout the empire, with the increasing popularity of inhumation. The marble for this sarcophagus came from Carrara in northern Italy, and for some cities, islands and regions the export of high-quality marble blocks for sarcophagi and other monuments became a mainstay of the economy. Some elements of the funeral such as the hired mourners, the funeral procession, banquets and the sarcophagus were very expensive, so many Romans joined burial clubs to provide a suitable funeral for themselves and their families.

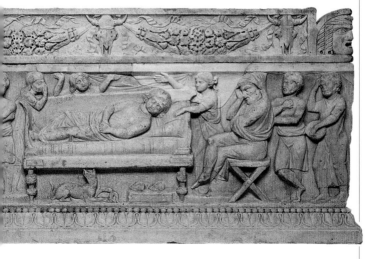

GLADIATOR'S HELMET

1ST CENTURY AD

This bronze helmet, said to have been found in the gladiators' barracks at Pompeii, has a grille of linked circles to protect the face, while a broad brim shields the back and sides of the head. At the front of the helmet is a medallion of Hercules, symbolising strength and victory. Although gladiators were sometimes slaves or criminals, many were professionals, trained to be a certain type of gladiator, for example the *Retiarius* armed with net and trident.

Gladiatorial games, originally performed at funerary rituals in Greek southern Italy, were brought to Rome in the fourth century BC, and became a popular form of mass-entertainment throughout the empire. Sponsoring the huge costs of the games could bestow great public acclaim and political benefits on local notables. Every major centre had an amphitheatre, the remains of which, as at Verona or Rome, are often among the most conspicuous reminders of their Roman past.

LAMP SHOWING A CHARIOT RACE

*c.*AD 175-225

The scene on this terracotta oil lamp almost certainly represents the Circus Maximus in Rome. Four-horsed chariots (*quadrigae*) charge left, urged on by the crowd, seen above left. Below the chariots is the central island (*spina*) of the stadium, adorned with statues, shrines, an obelisk and turning posts (*metae*).

Candles and lanterns were known in the Roman world, but metal or terracotta lamps which burned olive oil were far more popular. Huge quantities of mould-made terracotta lamps were mass-produced throughout the empire, in forms ranging from animals to objects such as boats and pine-cones. The most common lamp type had a flat, circular body, decorated with a wide range of different motifs: wildlife, deities, allegorical symbols, and scenes of everyday life. The manufacturer, SAECULUS, whose name is stamped on the base of this lamp, often featured gladiator or race scenes.

BUST OF THE EMPEROR ANTONINUS PIUS

AD 138-61

Antoninus Pius, Hadrian's adopted son, ruled in a period seen by many as a golden age, when the empire prospered behind its secure frontiers. The emperor is shown here in military uniform with a fringed cloak, fastened at the shoulder with a large fibula or brooch. He has a beard, moustache, and curly hair, a fashion started by Hadrian, which lasted into the later third century, when short hair again became fashionable.

This bust was one of several imperial portraits found in the ruins of the palatial town-house of Jason Magnus, in Cyrene, Libya. He and his family not only held key offices and sponsored public works in Cyrene, but also participated in the affairs of the empire, in particular those of the Greek-speaking eastern Mediterranean. As the empire grew and developed, local nobles such as Jason Magnus helped shift the focus of economic and political power from Italy to the provinces.

A GROUP OF FINE POTTERY TABLEWARE

1ST-3RD CENTURY AD

Throughout the empire most people used mass-produced, often mould-made, vessels of pottery or glass.

Three of the vases shown here are Red Slip Wares inspired by Hellenistic pottery from western Turkey: a large wine-bowl, made in Italy in the reign of Augustus and signed by Cnaeus Ateius; a dish from Tunisia of the fourth century AD, decorated with applied clay hounds and leaves; and a goblet made near Cologne in the mid-late second century, with piped barbotine decoration of a bird. The marbled bowl was made in the south of France in the reign of Nero, and the green-glazed cup was made between 50 BC - AD 50 in Turkey or Syria.

Pottery, generally not of great value, was exported in-amongst more valuable cargoes, such as corn, wine or olive oil, and is therefore a very useful indicator of trade, while its abundance and wide distribution reveal the enormous extent of the Mediterranean 'common market'.

GLASS JUG

c. AD 1–50

This elegant jug is a particularly fine example of blown glass. The mottled effect was created by blobs or chips of white glass which were picked up on a gather of brown glass and which then melted and extended to give a distinctive and attractive appearance as the piece was blown.

Glass was known for millennia before the Roman period, but it was only in the first century BC, after the invention of glass-blowing, perhaps in Syria or Palestine, that glass could became a common element in household tableware.

Workshops throughout the empire produced huge quantities of glass using the new technique. In Italy, glass workshops in cities such as Naples, Rome, Aquileia and Ravenna made a wide range of jars, bottles, bowls and dishes which were sometimes exported over great distances. This particular piece, made in northern Italy, was found in a tomb on one of the Greek islands.

SILVER TABLEWARE

2ND/3RD CENTURY AD

In wealthier Roman households, silver tableware was used. These pieces form part of a large hoard found near Chaourse in north-east France. The handled bowl was for mixing wine, the figurine of a squatting servant is a pepper-pot, and the serving-dish features a gilt figure of Mercury. The elegant jug is also partly gilt while the small bowl is decorated with bossing. Even the strainer/funnel is finely decorated.

The hoard was probably the accumulated wealth of a family, perhaps including Cavarianus and Genialis whose names are scratched on some pieces. It was buried in the second half of the third century, with many others, almost certainly in response to devastating barbarian raids on Roman France in the period. Raids and general unrest in the cities and countryside were symptomatic of the empire's general economic and military decline during the mid to late third century.

STATUE OF MITHRAS SLAYING THE BULL

2ND CENTURY AD

Mithras, whose cult originated in Persia, was one of the eastern deities including Cybele and Isis whose worship spread throughout the Roman empire during the second and third centuries AD. He is shown in eastern costume, including trousers and a Phrygian cap, killing a bull, whose blood symbolised the rebirth of light and life.

After secret initiation ceremonies, devotees graduated through ranks such as soldier, raven and, ultimately, father. They consumed bread and water (as the blood and meat of the bull) at communal meals, and this, with the religion's emphasis on regeneration, earned them the particular enmity of the Christians. Mithraism's popularity lay partly in its appeal to the army, but like all mystery religions, including Christianity, it benefited from ideological and philosophical changes in the late empire; these tended towards monotheism – the worship of a single god.

HINTON ST MARY MOSAIC

FIRST HALF OF 4TH CENTURY AD

This mosaic floor originally paved two rooms, the smaller section showing stag hunts, and Bellerophon slaying the chimaera, and the larger section with hunting scenes and seasons, separated by intricate borders. The central panel, illustrated here, shows a young, beardless man behind whose head are the Greek letters *chi* and *rho* – the first letters of the name of Christ and a recognised Christian symbol. The man is clearly intended to be Christ, of whom this is the earliest known representation from Britain, and one of the earliest from the empire as a whole. Its prominence in the centre of the mosaic reflects the religion's confidence following the emperor Constantine's conversion in the early fourth century.

The villa at Hinton St Mary probably controlled a large estate; similar villas throughout Britain show signs of refurbishment and expansion in the mid-fourth century, suggesting a period of stability and prosperity.

BRONZE GOOSE

This life-sized image of a goose was found on the site of the Hippodrome (the racing arena) at Istanbul in Turkey. Its function is uncertain, though the removable neck section and the pipe in the beak suggest it was more than a simple ornament. Perhaps it was a fountain spout, or even a mechanical device which could produce steam, smoke or even sound through its beak.

Byzantium, as the city was first called by its Greek founders, had been a prosperous though unremarkable provincial city in the early Roman empire. In the early fourth century, however, this changed because of the emperor Constantine's decision to make the city into a new imperial and Christian capital, which he renamed Constantinople. The city was transformed by a massive building programme of churches, palaces, public meeting-places, baths and other public structures, such as the Hippodrome.

THE MILDENHALL GREAT DISH

MID-4TH CENTURY AD

This outstanding salver, 60 cm across, of solid silver and weighing over 8 kg, is the most striking piece from a hoard of silver, including bowls, dishes and spoons, which was found near Mildenhall in Suffolk in the 1940s.

The decoration is pagan and is divided into three areas. At the centre is the head of the sea god Oceanus with dolphins emerging from his watery hair and beard, while around him a band of nymphs ride mythical sea-creatures. The main decoration shows Bacchus, Pan, Hercules and maenads (the female followers of Bacchus) and Satyrs (wild rustic beings recognisable by their pointed ears) celebrating a Bacchic ritual, complete with music and spirited dancing.

The hoard was buried in the early fifth century, and may reflect the unsettled period at the end of Roman rule as first the east of Britain, then the whole province, succumbed to raids and eventual settlement from overseas.

THE LYCURGUS CUP

This deep cup or chalice, a masterpiece of late Roman glass, was probably made in the Rhineland, though the silver-gilt mount and rim were added in the eighteenth century. The cup is a variation of the cage cup (*diatretum*) – made using a technique whereby a thick glass original was whittled away, leaving a design standing free of the background, linked to it only by struts, which were carefully concealed by the design. The scene shows the mythical Thracian king Lycurgus being strangled by vines as a punishment for threatening the god Bacchus and his followers.

The Lycurgus Cup is perhaps best known for its ability to change colour, from a deep pea-green under normal lighting conditions, to a rich magenta when light shines through it. This is a result of the presence of manganese and gold in the original glass mixture.

THE PROIECTA CASKET

LATE 4TH CENTURY AD

This silver casket for toiletries was part of a large hoard found on the Esquiline Hill in Rome in 1793. It is covered with embossed and partly gilt decoration showing mythological scenes including Venus and sea-nymphs, and others from real life: a woman dressing her hair, attended by servants. The central panel of the lid shows a couple flanked by cupids, and an inscription on the lid reading 'Secundus and Proiecta may you live in Christ' suggests that the casket formed part of a wedding gift. The weight of this generous gift, '22 pounds 3½ ounces', is also inscribed on the lid.

Records suggest Secundus may have belonged to a pagan family while Proiecta was a Christian, which would explain the juxtaposition of the Christian inscription with overtly pagan motifs. It is likely then that this piece was made for their wedding, during the period of relative religious tolerance in the 360s-70s.

IVORY PLAQUE

EARLY 5TH CENTURY AD

This plaque was originally one of a pair or diptych, which contained a waxed writing tablet. It shows the deification of a noble, who is seen on a carriage, drawn by elephants. Beyond, topped by the statue of a god in a chariot, is his funeral pyre, from which fly eagles representing his soul. Finally, carried to heaven by two winds, he is greeted by his ancestors.

Ivory carving flourished in the later empire, and great craftman's skill can be seen in the detail and quality of the carving, for example the elephant trainers with their ball-like rattles, and the chariot on the funeral pyre. The 'patchwork' effect on the elephants was the normal way of showing their leathery skin in Roman art.

The monogram SYMMACHORUM at the top of the panel suggests the noble was one of the Symmachi, an important senatorial family from Rome, which led the pagan faction's struggle against the growing power of Christianity.

ACCESSION NUMBERS OF OBJECTS ILLUSTRATED

First published in 1996 by British Museum Press
A division of The British Museum Company Ltd
46 Bloomsbury Street, London WC1B 3QQ

A catalogue record for this book is available from the British Library

ISBN 0-7141-2111-8

Text by Paul Roberts
Photography by British Museum Photographic Service
Designed by Butterworth Design

Typeset in Garamond
Manufactured in China
by Imago Publishing Ltd

Jacket illustration: Small panel from a large mosaic floor,
showing dolphins flanking a trident, 4th century BC.

Frontispiece: Base-disc of the Portland Vase, showing Paris,
Prince of Troy, deciding who was the most beautiful of the
three goddesses, Aphrodite, Athena and Hera.